Little Liverpool

Diaries

SUSAN LIVERPOOL

faith books & MORE

Suwanee, GA

PHOTOGRAPHED BY JAMES HILL

First published by Faith Books & MORE
ISBN 978-0-9842378-9-0

Printed in the United States of America.

This book is printed on acid-free paper.

James Hill, Photographer
www.jamesadamhill.com

Edited by
Gloria Spencer

Graphic Designer
Bridgett Burchfield

3255 Lawrenceville-Suwanee Rd.
Suite P250
Suwanee, GA 30024
publishing@faithbooksandmore.com
www.faithbooksandmore.com

Dedication

This book is written in honor of my family and
dedicated to my Grandparents and all
Grandparents.

It is also lovingly dedicated to my wonderful
son,
Jason Alexander Hill

and
to all my ancestors, who have gone before, who
paved the way and surround me now.

I am because you were!

Acknowledgements

There are so many people that touched this project with their love and support. They are part of my Community, my "Family."

I love and thank each one of you.
You are a treasure and blessing in my life!

Joe Hampton
Phoebe Bailey
Liz Allen
Ann Wilson
Linda Anderson
Wilma Kirchhofer
Angelyn Wright
Bobbie Wright
Teresa Hampton
Valerie Andrews
Verna Barksdale
Ernie Brazeal
Barbara Day
Angenetta Crayton
Phyllis McCall
Ramona Dorsey
Eugene Harrington
Rod Pass
Karen Strothers

Joan Lowman
Tedi May
JoAnn Fuller
Claudette Romious
Windy Williams
Chuck Beasley
John Tsvarasis
Risa Berlin
Adrianne Kiernan
Kathy Chiu
Pat Fiorello
Collins Phillips
Janice Daniel Hill
Aretha Booker
Wanda Terrell
Irma Walker and "Diamond"
Alice Sanders
Susan Campis

Special Acknowledgements

Thank you for what you brought to each and every
photograph

DeAnna Parks Jones - "Grandmommy"
Sheye Breaux - "Granddaddy"
Sherita Daniels - "Mommy"
Tamera Daniels - Susan Diane "Little Liverpool"

and

To my Financial Patrons

It takes a Village and it definitely takes some money!
Thank you

Angelyn Wright
Liz Allen

Table of Contents

Foreword by

Joe Hampton

It is not often that one can participate in the making of a masterpiece. Almost from the beginning of The Little Liverpool Diaries, I have had the opportunity to witness ART at work in transforming both the writer and the reader. I saw these stories arrive to the author as if they were gifts from God. The stories seemed to channel through her already whole and complete, needing very little editing or recomposing to bring immediate joy and healing.

The process of making this work available to the general public has already made a powerful impact upon the people who worked to make it happen. We have a new respect for the ancestors in our lives who have gone before. Through the gift of these stories, we have a deeper appreciation for the mothers, fathers and grandparents in our lives.

Truth is larger than fiction. It embraces the best in us. May you experience what is yours to cherish as you partake of the gifts you are going to receive from this book.

Joe Hampton, MSW

Foreword by
Phoebe Lydia Bailey

Whether you grew up in the 50s, in the Midwest, or as a "colored girl" in the south, you will find a connection to the stories of Susan Diane Liverpool. Young readers can appreciate the universal struggle to enter and understand the world of adults. As an adult reader, I share in Susan Diane Liverpool's recognition of the growth of wisdom from naïveté.

All former children may remember a time when they first heard an adult say something they had been told was forbidden as in Susan Diane's "Introduction to Cursing." As a child, did you ever have the satisfaction of an adult apologizing to you? Savor, "The Truth Will Set You Free." Then there is the pain of the first encounter with racism in, "Fistfight."

I won't give them all away. But here's a caution: you may want to put on an extra pair of underwear before you begin reading. I confess that I have laughed so hard I almost wet my pants!

Phoebe Lydia Bailey, PhD
Educator and Corporate Coach

Introduction

The journey to the creation of this book begins with my family. I am a blessed human being. I was never sexually, physically or verbally abused. I was never mistreated or neglected. I was simply loved and spoiled.

All the stories you are about to read are true. The events actually happened to me except for the body falling out of the casket, in the story "Funerals, Wakes and Other Social Events." I embellished just a little in that one.

In my community on the Southside of Chicago, being an only child was a difficult experience during a time when it was rare to be without siblings and even rarer to have a name like Susan Diane Liverpool, for goodness' sake!

As Grandmommy would say, "What 'colored girl' is named Susan?" I can thank my father now for my last name, (he was born in Georgetown, British Guyana, South America) but back then I hated it. I didn't want to be different; I wanted desperately to fit in. The 1950s were times of turmoil and change in Chicago. To my family's credit, they did the best they could to shield me from harm, to love me and to provide a safe, nurturing environment.

This book is a tribute to their memory. I have always felt I never said thank you enough to them. I am sure they are smiling down from heaven.

So… to Mattie Lou (Grandmommy), Ezekiel Hawk (Granddaddy) and Dorothy Thomas (Mommy), I say a loving…Thank you!

One

Me, Grandmommy,
the '52 Packard and
My Introduction
to Cursing

Me, Grandmommy, the '52 Packard and My Introduction to Cursing

My grandmommy refused to call me Susan. She always used my middle name, Diane. Grandmommy would say, "I don't know why your mother even named you Susan. Ain't no colored girls named Susan." She was right. I didn't know any colored girls named Susan either.

Grandmommy and I were like two peas in a pod. She took me everywhere she went and boy did I love it! I got to see all kinds of "stuff." I just knew, by the time I started kindergarten, the "stuff" I was seeing was gonna put me way ahead of the other kids. She and my granddaddy owned an olive green 1952 Packard. I loved that car and I especially loved riding in it with Grandmommy.

There was only one problem going places with Grandmommy though; she drove as slow as molasses. I'd slide way down in my seat 'cause I didn't want anybody to know I was with the slowest driving person in the entire world!

"Grandmommy, why do you have to drive so slow? Everybody's passing us!"

"I don't care, let 'em pass me. They ain't gettin' there no sooner by driving fast, and I ain't gonna kill myself tryin' to keep up with them." On and on she'd go. It was no use arguing with her, she wasn't gonna drive any faster.

It was a small price to pay for a chance to go for a ride. Only my eyes would be visible as I peered out of the car window watching all the other cars zoom past us honking their horns and waving their fists, especially that middle finger.

It was a warm sunny day and I don't remember where we were going. All I know is that we were making a left turn in that big old Packard. I was leaning against the passenger door looking out the window like I always did when all of a sudden, as Grandmommy

was making her turn, the passenger door flew open!

Since I was already holding onto the door handle, I just kept hanging on for dear life. Wow, this was fun! I couldn't believe it. I, Little Liverpool, was hanging out of the car, holding onto the door handle. I was suddenly a daredevil like on TV. No, I was a trapeze artist. No, I was Annie Oakley hanging onto my horse. There I was with the road whizzing along below me and the warm breeze whipping all around me. Wheeee! Look at me! I'm riding on the outside of a moving car!

Then suddenly, I was jerked back to reality by the sound of Grandmommy screaming at the top of her lungs. She was frantically holding onto my leg with one hand and steering the car to a stop with the other. That's probably the only thing that saved me from becoming road kill. Uh-oh, I thought to myself. I'm in trouble now. She's never gonna believe I didn't do this on purpose.

Finally, Grandmommy brought the car to a stop and pulled me back in. My brush with death and fame were over. That was fun. What an adventure! I slowly and cautiously turned to look at

Grandmommy and braced myself for a lickin'. To my surprise, she was holding her hand over her heart, breathing heavily and saying, "Oh, Jesus, oh Lordy, oh Jesus," over and over. Then came the moment that changed my life forever. My Grandmommy said a curse word! Oooowee! I was beside myself with glee. My Grandmommy was human! I was gonna milk this baby for all it was worth. I turned to face Grandmommy and did my best to look surprised and shocked. "Grandmommy, you said a bad word! You said, 'X?OX!'"

When Grandmommy finally caught her breath, she turned to me and said, "I know, I know I said a bad word. Now, don't you go tellin' your momma, you hear me? Please don't do that, okay? And for goodness sake, Diane, please don't tell her you almost fell out of the car!"

Grandmommy was begging! I knew this because her tone had softened, which was unlike grandmommy. My grandmommy had what people back then called a "fiery" temper. She always said what was on her mind, and she never minced words, so this sudden change in her tone of voice could only mean one thing: she was really worried about what might happen if this story got back to my mother who could also be very scary.

So I decided this might be a good time to start crying, I scrunched up my face and began crying and sobbing. My plan was to keep Grandmommy from thinking I had pulled this stunt on purpose.

As it turned out, I didn't need to worry about that. She blamed herself and promised God she would devote her life to becoming a better grandmother.

So being the cunning Little Liverpool that I was, I remembered that she had been thinking about making my favorite dessert that evening, lemon meringue pie. So I said in my sweetest Little Liverpool voice, "Grandmommy, if I don't tell Mommy about this will you make that lemon meringue pie tonight?"

"Yes baby, Grandmommy will make that lemon meringue pie just for you, but only if you don't tell your mommy what happened today, okay?"

"Okay, I promise Grandmommy, I won't tell. It'll be our little secret."

"That's right baby, this is our little secret between you and me. Nobody else needs to know that I almost killed my grandbaby! Oh Lord have mercy, oh, Jesus!" She started up again as she closed her eyes and leaned back in her seat trying to compose herself. Grandmommy was "sweatin' like a mule" (one of her favorite expressions). I reached in her pocketbook and handed her the favorite perfumed handkerchief she always carried which she promptly used to wipe away the sweat from her face and bosom.

How happy I was! In one day I had managed not only to have an exciting adventure but also to blackmail Grandmommy into making her world-famous lemon meringue pie for dessert. All was right with the world.

Dinner was always an event at our house. Everyone had their

own special place. Granddaddy was always at the head of the table, Grandmommy and I sat side by side and Mommy held down the other end of the table. My grandparents were both great cooks, but it was Grandmommy who did most of the cooking and boy, oh boy, could she go to town in that kitchen.

So there we were quietly enjoying our meal, all of us engrossed in our own thoughts. Suddenly, my mother turns to me and says, "So Susan, what did you do today?"

At first I just kept eating. Then suddenly the joy of that car ride came rushing back to me and without thinking I blurted, "Oh, mommy, guess what happened to me and grandmommy?"

"What, sweetie?" my mother asked.

At that precise moment, there was loud coughing at the table. But being just six years old, I didn't hear this as my cue to shut up.

I just figured something had gotten caught in Grandmommy's throat.

"Mommy," I continued, "I almost fell out of the car today and Grandmommy said, 'X?OX!'"

I quickly put my hand over my mouth as if that would suck the words back in. But it was too late. There it was, the whole story, out there floating over the kitchen table like fog. Everybody's mouths were wide open, their forks poised in midair. You could have heard a pin drop. I hung my head and continued eating, not daring to look up at anyone. I was horrified! I had broken my promise to my beloved grandmommy. I had "hung her out to dry!" I had left her "twisting in the wind." You get the picture. I don't know what happened after that. I just remember feeling the mood at the table grow heavy and dark like an approaching storm. I kept my face near my plate and continued to shovel in my dinner.

After what seemed an eternity, Grandmommy said, "Who wants some lemon meringue pie?"

I was afraid to look up, but my desire to have some pie got the best of me. I slowly raised my head to see that Grandmommy was glaring a hole right through me. If looks could kill, I'd have been dead in my chair. I did get my lemon meringue pie but it just didn't taste as yummy as I had anticipated. Still, Grandmommy forgave me and continued to love and adore me. As she would say some years later, "If there's something you want to keep a secret, definitely do not tell Diane!"

Two

Grandmommy,
the Rock and the
Squirrel

Grandmommy, the Rock and the Squirrel

It was a hot, muggy, lazy summer afternoon. Grandmommy and I were having a good time just leaning over the back porch railing, gazing down on her beautiful vegetable garden. Grandmommy loved her garden. She was growing collard greens, tomatoes and watermelons. I loved standing next to Grandmommy, leaning over the second floor railing. Now, Mommy didn't like me leaning over that railing. It made her nervous. She said it was dangerous. So leaning over the railing became a secret between Grandmommy and me.

Suddenly, from behind the bushes popped this cute little bushy-tailed squirrel with eyes as big as walnuts. I couldn't tell if he was eating something or biting his nails; he seemed very jumpy. He was eyeing Grandmommy's garden. He'd inch his way closer and closer, stopping every few seconds to look this way and that. The closer he got to the garden the faster his tail fluttered.

This squirrel had to be crazy or from out of town or both because it was well known in the local squirrel community that my grandmommy was nuts about her garden. If she saw a squirrel go anywhere near her garden she'd start to curse, holler, call on the Lord and throw whatever she could get her hands on until they were frightened away. Eventually, the squirrels and Grandmommy came to an understanding. They would play and scamper around the yard avoiding the garden and Grandmommy would leave them alone.

So that's why I say this squirrel had to be crazy or from out of town, because once he saw the coast was clear, he scurried over to those collard greens just as bold as you please and began munching away as fast as his little jaws could chew.

When Grandmommy spotted this little rebel she began calling on the Almighty Lord Jesus. I half expected the heavens to open up and zap the poor thing. Unfortunately for him, I wasn't far off.

Grandmommy frantically looked around for something to scare him with before he could eat more of the beloved collard greens. She found a large rock in a nearby flower pot, grabbed it and taking quick aim, threw it at the squirrel hoping to scare it away.

You won't believe what happened next. Even we couldn't believe what happened next. The rock hit that poor little squirrel dead center in the head. Mr. Squirrel fell over in a heap. The only blessing out of the whole thing was that he probably never knew what hit him.

Grandmommy and I were speechless! We leaned way over the railing now! We were trying to see if what we thought had just happened, really had happened. We just knew he couldn't be dead. He was probably stunned and would soon "come to" and wobble away with a really bad headache. But he didn't move at all and after a while Grandmommy and I realized Mr. Squirrel was never gonna move.

Finally, it was I that broke the silence. "Grandmommy! You killed it. You killed that poor little squirrel. What are you going to do now?"

Grandmommy let out a long sigh. I knew that soon she'd be calling on the Lord. Sure enough, Grandmommy began to cry out.

"Lord have mercy, I just meant to scare the poor thing!"

Slowly and carefully she started down the stairs, stopping every few steps to catch her breath. There I was, right behind her, badgering her all the way. "Grandmommy, do you think it's dead? Did you kill it? What are you going to do with it?" I'm sure at that moment nothing would have pleased her more than to stuff a rag in my mouth. Anything to shut me up!

Finally, we made it down to the yard and I, being faster of course, raced around Grandmommy and hurried over to see the dead-as-a-doornail Mr. Squirrel. I had never seen anything dead before. What an exciting day this had turned out to be!

I drew closer to get a good look and heard Grandmommy shriek from behind me, "Diane, don't touch it! Get away! Let me see it first."

I obeyed, mainly because the closer I got the more afraid I became. I didn't know if I was really ready to see this dead thing. Grandmommy

made her way over to the dearly and newly departed Mr. Squirrel from parts unknown. She was out of breath and "sweatin' like a mule."

She used her cane to poke it and push it. No response. Nothing. We both stood there quietly staring down at poor Mr. Squirrel. Finally, it was Grandmommy who broke the silence this time as she continued to gaze at the squirrel. "Diane, you don't need to go blabbing this around to everybody," and by "everybody" we both knew she meant my mommy. We also knew from past experience that it was not possible for me to keep a secret. "At least you don't have to say I murdered the poor thing."

"Murder? What's murder Grandmommy?"

Grandmommy muttered under her breath, "Oh Lord, I should've kept my mouth shut." Then to me she said, "All I'm saying Diane, is that Grandmommy didn't mean to kill the squirrel; it was an accident, okay?" But she knew it was too late. I kept asking her what the word murder meant. Was that the same as killing something?

Grandmommy told me to run upstairs and fetch an empty shoe box and bring the dust pan. She scooped up the squirrel and put him in the shoe box then placed it all in the garbage can. She pulled some matches from her pockets, (she kept everything in her pockets) lit the match and dropped it into the garbage can.

Next she told me to bring the garden hose around. Before the flames could get out of control, she doused them with water. I asked her how she knew to do all these things and was that the right way to get rid of a dead Mr. Squirrel. She didn't answer. When Grandmommy stopped answering my questions, I knew I had pushed her to the edge and it was time to "hush my mouth," as she loved to say.

Surprisingly, Mr. Squirrel started to smell like some kind of meat cooking. On TV westerns I had seen cowboys eating squirrel meat over a campfire. I wondered why we didn't just take it upstairs and barbeque it like the cowboys did. But I knew better than to ask that question. Grandmommy had that look on her face as if she was about to go off the deep end. She was probably worried about what was gonna come out of my mouth at the table that night.

The mood at dinner was very quiet. We were all at our places enjoying our meal. Wouldn't you just know it; we were having collard greens. I used my fork to carefully separate the greens from the rest of my food. I just couldn't bring myself to eat them. Every time I looked at those greens I thought about that poor dead squirrel. I could feel Granddaddy and Mommy watching me with curiosity 'cause I was never this quiet at the table. I usually hummed as I ate because it just seemed to make my food taste better.

Finally, Granddaddy spoke. This was always an event because Granddaddy was a man of few words. "Baby, what's the matter?"

Before I could open my mouth, Grandmommy startled everybody by yelling, "Who's ready for watermelon? Granddaddy, why don't you get the watermelon out of the refrigerator? Diane, come on now, grab your mommy's plate and help me clear away the dishes."

Grandmommy was trying to distract everybody. I figured that out a few years later. You see, my mommy and my grandmommy would argue with each other about me. Grandmommy was just gettin' out of the "dog house" for some other trouble she and I had gotten into before. So Grandmommy wasn't quite ready to jump back in over having "murdered" a squirrel.

Mommy and Granddaddy looked at Grandmommy, then back at each other. They knew she was creating a distraction and they knew it probably had to do with some fiasco that involved the two of us. So I did as I was told and prepared for one of my most favorite things in the whole wide world: eating watermelon.

As we slurped our cold sweet dessert, I thought about how good a watermelon from the garden tastes, nothing like a store-bought one. Ah, yes... watermelon from the garden...the garden! "Mommy, guess what Grandmommy did today? She murdered a squirrel. She hit him square in the head with a rock from right up here on the back porch. You should have seen him. He fell over dead, just like this." I plunked my head on the table with a thud for dramatic effect. "Then she burned him in the garbage can."

The very next moment I realized I was supposed to have kept this a secret between me and Grandmommy. I looked over at Grandmommy to find her staring at me with this strange look on her face. It was as if she wanted to say something to me but was doing everything she could to hold her tongue.

At that moment I realized it was time for me to give up on being a secret keeper. It just wasn't working out.

Suddenly, everyone began snickering, then laughing hysterically. Instead of being upset about the poor dead squirrel, they were laughing at how funny I was. I, Little Liverpool, had made my family laugh. I was so proud of myself and feeling very important thank you. So for the time being at least, Grandmommy and I were still out of the "dog house" and ready for our next adventure.

Three

So Where's the Car?

So Where's the Car?

Well, as I said before, my family owned an olive green '52 Packard. I really loved that car. It was my home away from home. If I wasn't looking out the window watching the world go by, I was curled up on the front seat next to Grandmommy or Granddaddy, depending on who was driving, or in the back seat either taking a nap or just stretched out gazing up at the sky. Back then there were no seatbelts to worry about, so riding in a car was kinda like being on a moving sofa.

Lots of times when Granddaddy was driving he'd let me sit on his lap and I'd help him "drive" the car. This was so much fun and it was our little secret, because if Mommy and Grandmommy had found out they would have had a fit! But where was the fun in sitting on Granddaddy's lap when the car was parked? I needed to "help" Granddaddy drive! I'd giggle and steer the wheel saying,

"Look Granddaddy, I'm driving the car!" Now, watching the road wasn't my problem, I was busy talking to Granddaddy.

I also spent a lot of time trying to figure out what my family was talking about. When they didn't want me to know what they were saying, they'd spell it instead of saying it. This was very annoying because I couldn't spell that well and when it came to big words, well, forget it! I knew they were talking about a car. That was an easy word. But there were other words I didn't know, such as "deal-er-ship." What was a deal-er-ship?

We'd all be sitting around the kitchen table having dinner or something and suddenly somebody would spell out a word. My ears would perk up and I'd say, "Hey, what was that word?"

They'd keep talking as if they hadn't heard me. I knew they heard me 'cause I knew how to be loud. You had to be loud in my family to get a word in edge-wise.

Sooner or later, I'd give up and go back to eating or doing whatever else I was doing, dreaming of the day when I'd be able to spell better. Then I'd know everything!

One day after church, instead of going home, we all drove to this big place where there were lots of cars sitting outside like at a parking lot. All the cars were so clean and shiny. Some even had whitewall tires. I didn't know why we were there, so I found ways to keep myself company while Granddaddy, Grandmommy and Mommy went to talk to this funny-looking man who wore thick glasses. Something big must be happening. We didn't usually do big things on Sunday.

Soon I was bored and ready to go. I had emptied my new pocketbook ten times and put everything back in ten times. I loved my new pocketbook. It was just for Sundays and it was just the right size. I could wear it on my arm like I'd seen some of the big girls do or I could swing it from my hand which was my favorite way to carry it. Having a pocketbook meant I was almost grown.

Finally! We were leaving but we weren't headed toward "our"

car. "Granddaddy?" I asked, "Where's the car?"

Everybody just kept walking. Nobody answered my question. Then the funny-looking man with the thick glasses began laughing. He bent down close to me and said, "What's your name, honey?"

I just stared at him. Why was he talking to me? The fact that I didn't answer wasn't a problem for him. He just kept on talking.

"Well little lady, your granddaddy just bought a brand new car and we're gonna take that old Packard off your hands. Isn't that nice?"

I looked up at Granddaddy just in time to see him turn his head away from me. Granddaddy didn't like to say no to me or give me bad news; he left that up to Grandmommy and Mommy. So I looked over at them. They rolled their eyes at each other as if they knew trouble was comin'.

"Granddaddy, we're not gonna have the Packard anymore?"

Tears were already streaming down my face. Grandmommy pushed her way between me and the funny-looking man, almost knocking him over. His glasses went sideways as he tried to look around Grandmommy and continue to talk to me.

"That's right little lady. But you don't want that old car anymore now do you? You're gonna have a brand new car!"

Grandmommy was not a woman who knew how to pretend to be nice. She glared at the funny-looking man and said, "Mister, we'll handle this!" Then she turned to me. She took a deep breath and said, "Diane, it was time for us to buy a new car, okay? That Packard was old and on its last leg."

By now I was sobbing as I thought about all the good times in that old Packard. "What's gonna happen to the car Grandmommy?"

Before Grandmommy could answer, the funny-looking man again tried to butt in and help. "Don't you worry sweetheart. We're gonna find a nice home for that car." He pointed and I followed his finger. There was the beloved old Packard being driven around to the back of the lot.

I broke away from Grandmommy and ran toward the car yelling, "Bring it back! Bring it back! That's my car!"

Now Grandmommy was "fit to be tied" (one of her favorite expressions) as she spun around to face mister "funny-looking man," giving him her, "why couldn't you just keep your big mouth shut," looks.

Mister funny-looking man turned beet-red as he stared at Grandmommy and began to slowly back away. He cleared his throat and said, "Uh, well, if there's nothing else, folks, I gotta get back to work. You folks have a nice day now and enjoy that new car." Then he turned and hurried back to his office.

By now a crowd had gathered as they watched my granddaddy scoop me up and carry me kicking and screaming away from the Packard. Grandmommy and Mommy were right behind him straightening their clothes after helping to wrestle me away from my beloved old car.

Granddaddy set me down and leaned against the new car,

trying to catch his breath. The three of them had me hemmed in so I couldn't escape. "Lord have mercy," Grandmommy said as she frowned at me then glanced around to see who was still watching this circus. "She's okay. She left her teddy bear in the old car." This seemed to satisfy the questioning looks on people's faces and the crowd quickly broke up. Then Mommy, Grandmommy and Granddaddy crossed their arms and glared silently down at me.

I wasn't scared. I was ready for 'em. I crossed my arms, too, and poked out my bottom lip. It was Mommy that spoke, barely above a whisper. Her tone was as cold as ice cubes. It was her "I mean business" voice. "Diane, you will get in this new car and not another word had better come out of your mouth. Do you hear me?"

"Yes, ma'am," I whispered as I stared down at my shoes. When mommy sounded like that there was no use fighting anymore.

The ride home was very quiet. Most of the way no one said a word. How could this be happening? Why didn't they tell me they were going to get rid of the Packard? And I didn't like this new car anyway. It smelled funny, plus it was dark blue. Grownups! They just did whatever they wanted. They didn't care how you felt about it. But I'd show them. I would never ride in this ol'new car again. Suddenly, I heard music! It was coming from the front. This car had a radio? Wow! I jumped up and leaned over the seat, resting my head between Granddaddy and Grandmommy. "This car has a radio Granddaddy?"

"That's right baby. You like it?"

I didn't say anything at first. I just let the music carry me away. After a while I said, "It's okay." Then I slid back into my seat and began to hum along with the music.

"'Cause if you don't like it now, Granddaddy can take it back and get that old Packard again."

I saw Granddaddy turn to Grandmommy and Mommy and give them a wink. I knew what he was doing so I played along.

"That's okay Granddaddy. You can keep this one."

"Thank you baby. I sure appreciate that!" I loved my granddaddy. He really knew how to treat a lady.

26

FOUR

Funerals, Wakes and Other Social Events

Funerals, Wakes and Other Social Events

It was the fall of 1955. I was too young for Kindergarten so when I wasn't playing with my friends I spent all my time with my grandparents, and that was just fine by me.

Plus, I had a secret life. My grandmommy loved to take me places and one of the places she'd take me on a regular basis was to somebody's funeral or wake. Yes, I said "somebody's" because it didn't matter that the "dearly departed" wasn't a close friend or family member. They had died in our community and that was good enough for Grandmommy and her merry band of friends.

At first I didn't like going to these funerals and wakes. (Mostly we went to wakes because it would have been impolite to go to the funeral of someone we didn't know very well.) The flowers smelled funny and the organ music always sounded so sad. But it was fun to watch all the shouting, screaming, jumping, fainting and "falling out" that went on at these things.

Sometimes it was scary watching all that drama. But I knew when it was over there was gonna be some good eatin' in the Fellowship Hall or basement of the church. This, too, was a tradition in our community. Any wake worth its salt was always followed by a mouth-watering reception. Everyone was expected to bring a home-cooked dish. So during the service, I'd sit patiently next to Grandmommy and imagine all the aromas and flavors of the wonderful dishes that awaited me.

Now, at this point in the story, you might be thinking to yourself, that poor child, being dragged around to all those morbid events by her grandmother. Shame on that woman! What was she thinking? But as far as I was concerned, it was a chance for me to go places with Grandmommy and see stuff.

The family spirit that surrounded these gatherings always made me feel happy. Once you got used to the drama it was pretty okay and like I said, that good home-cooked food made it all worthwhile. I would eat to my heart's content.

Mommy didn't like the fact that Grandmommy took me to so many wakes, but what was she going to do, hire a babysitter? Think about it. Who was going to take better care of me than my own grandmommy? We were a tiny family and as quirky as Grandmommy could be, she was more normal than a lot of folks. So Mommy put up with it, and to their credit, I seem to have turned out okay.

One of these wakes stands out in my memory more than the others. We went because Grandmommy was good friends with the sister of the niece of the brother of the uncle of the dearly departed. That was a good enough connection to get an invite.

One thing you always did was to go up and "view" the deceased. This ritual amazed me. It was kind of like slowing down to gawk at an accident, dreading but hoping you might see some blood and guts. Grandmommy never forced me to go with her to view the person. I usually stayed in my seat until she returned, but I was always torn between going to look and staying put.

At this particular wake I overheard Grandmommy and her friends talking about how young the deceased girl was. That did it! I knew I had to see her. I had never seen a deceased young person before. Why had she died so young? What would she look like?

I told Grandmommy I wanted to go up and see the body. She surprised me by asking why. I was quick on my feet though and said, "I think I know her."

I think I know her? Where had that come from? I was impressed with my fast response, and again, to my surprise, Grandmommy said okay. So I took her hand and we joined the viewing line.

I was scared and excited all at the same time. As we got closer to the casket I thought I might chicken out but I didn't. Finally we were there. I stood on my toes but I wasn't tall enough to see inside

the casket. I was overwhelmed with the urge to touch this girl. I just couldn't believe she was really dead. I had to see for myself. If I could just get close enough to touch her chest I could tell if she was breathing or not.

I cautiously looked around. Grandmommy was talking to the lady standing next to her. "They did a good job with her, don't you think?"

"Yes, indeed. She looks like she did in life."

What a funny thing to say about a dead person! But time was a-wasting and I had to act fast.

I took a deep breath, reached into the casket and felt around until my hand brushed against her chest. Wow! She was as hard as a rock. But I still wasn't satisfied. I needed to see. I wanted to see if she was breathing or not. I was gonna have to get closer. But how? Then I noticed that the casket was on a stand and the stand was covered by a purple drape. If I could somehow balance my foot on that stand I could see into the casket.

I looked around at Grandmommy. She was still talking with

that lady. Now was the time! I carefully placed one foot on the stand then the other. The stand began to wobble a little but that was okay. I could just about see over the edge of the casket. I carefully leaned in closer to get a good look at the dead girl. Oh! She was so pretty! Why, she wasn't dead. She was probably just asleep. I bet if I simply whispered her name she would open her eyes and say hi.

Suddenly I heard Grandmommy scream. "Diane! What are you doing?"

Hearing Grandmommy call my name scared me so bad I lost my balance. Then suddenly the casket started to tilt. Grandmommy was pulling me away before I could let go. Next thing I knew everything went into slow motion, like in the movies. Grandmommy had me and I had the casket. It came tumbling off the podium and the dead girl rolled onto the floor. Everyone was watching but nobody seemed to be able to move. Grandmommy let out a strange moan and said, "Oh, Lord, have mercy!" Then she fainted dead away into the arms of the lady she had been talking to.

Since Grandmommy was still holding on to me, I went down on top of her and the dead girl was right beside us. This all happened very quickly, but it seemed to take forever. The organ music had stopped. You could have heard a pin drop! All eyes were on the pile of bodies (living and dead) on the floor. Several of the ushers, with their white-gloved hands, sprang into action. Their job was to stand around waiting for just this sort of drama. They quickly began fanning Grandmommy and wiping her forehead. Meanwhile, the deacons struggled to get the dead girl back into her coffin. This wasn't easy because she was as stiff as a board.

Then I noticed the strangest thing. Nobody seemed the least bit phased by what was happening. People were acting like this sort of thing happened all the time. Everyone figured that Grandmommy had been overcome with grief. It was perfectly understandable!

Of course Grandmommy would play along with this 'cause she

didn't want anybody to know it was her very own granddaughter that had knocked over the casket and started this circus in the first place.

I, on the other hand, was speechless. I had never seen anybody faint before, let alone my very own grandmommy! My eyes were as big as saucers. Everybody was looking down at Grandmommy saying, "Bless her heart."

Suddenly, the thought occurred to me that maybe my grandmommy was dying right here at this wake. I burst into tears, buried my head in her bosom and started sobbing hysterically saying, "Grandmommy, grandmommy, please don't die!" The lady ushers pulled me off Grandmommy and tried to calm me down. "Alright now baby settle down, your grandmommy's gonna be just fine. She just fainted, that's all. Don't you worry now, she's gonna come to any minute."

I began to quiet down but then I started thinkin'; if she's not dead, then she's gonna kill me.

Slowly, Grandmommy's eyelids began to flutter. She looked around as if trying to remember where she was. Then she saw me standing over her, holding the hand of one of the ushers. Grandmommy closed her eyes again, moaning and shaking her head back and forth.

"Somebody get her some water," one of the ushers said as they started fanning her a little faster.

Finally, after many goodbyes, "Are you sure you're alright?"s and "Are you sure you can drive?"s, someone said, "Mattie, why don't you let us call your husband so he can come take you and Diane home?"

"No! No, that's alright, everybody, we'll be fine. Y'all don't need to do that. Come on, Diane, let's go." Grandmommy grabbed my hand and away we flew toward the car. My feet barely touched the ground. I was hardly in my seat good before Grandmommy screeched that car away from the curb, leaving a cloud of smoke between us and the small group of people watching us drive away.

I had never seen Grandmommy drive that fast before.

During the ride home, neither one of us said a word. You could have cut the tension with a knife. Finally, Grandmommy broke the silence. "Diane?"

"Yes, Grandmommy?" I could tell by the tone of her voice this was gonna be bad.

"Do you want to keep goin' places with Grandmommy or are you ready for me to put you in nursery school?"

I knew what that meant. If I blabbed to my mommy about what happened today it would be the end of the road for me, Grandmommy and my chance to get out and see stuff. If Mommy knew that not only was I being hauled around to a lot more wakes and funerals lately, but now I was knocking dead people out of their caskets, she'd have a conniption! (That's a fancy word for being really upset.)

This called for an Academy Award winning performance. I turned on the tears full force. "No, Grandmommy please! I don't want to go to nursery school! I won't tell mommy what happened today, I promise! Please Grandmommy, don't send me to nursery school!"

I could have saved my breath 'cause Grandmommy seemed to be ignoring me. I had blabbed so many other secrets, why should she believe me now? All I could hope was that Grandmommy's desire to have me around would override her desire to send me away. After all, we were a team, two peas in a pod and she would miss me terribly if I went off to nursery school. Well, that's the story I told myself anyway.

I looked up at Grandmommy with reddened eyes and tear-stained cheeks, but she continued to stare straight ahead, tightly gripping that steering wheel. She was working her jaw like she did when she was worried about something. I knew it was best to leave her alone. I had done all I could.

That night, Grandmommy fixed all my favorite foods. Fried chicken, macaroni and cheese, collard greens, corn bread and peach cobbler with vanilla ice cream – strawberry ice cream for Granddaddy, 'cause that was his favorite. I'm sure Grandmommy hoped making this special dinner would be enough to keep me quiet.

So there we were, all gathered around the table – me, Granddaddy, Mommy and Grandmommy – quietly enjoying our dinner. Then my mother asked the dreaded question. "So, Susan, what did you do today?"

I opened my mouth to speak when suddenly Grandmommy began humming one of her favorite songs, "What a Friend We Have in Jesus," as she rose from the table to get more iced tea from the refrigerator.

Uh oh! Somehow I knew that was my cue to shut up! "Nothing," I said.

"Nothing?" Mommy replied.

Grandmommy's humming was getting louder by the minute!

Of course Mommy and Granddaddy had forgotten all about me by now and were staring at Grandmommy as if to say, what in the world is going on with all this humming?

Grandmommy calmly returned to the table, finished her humming, flashed everybody a big smile then turned to me. "Diane, you mean to tell me you're not going to tell your mommy what happened today?"

I began to cough and choke as my food went down the "wrong pipe." I stared at Grandmommy in disbelief. Terror seized my body. I couldn't believe it. Was she about to rat me out? This couldn't be happening! I could see nursery school looming over me like a tornado ready to sweep me away.

"You remember," she said in this kind of sweet syrupy voice that I had never heard from her before. "You and I went to visit my friend, Ms. Mable, and she gave you your first piece of sponge cake.

Remember, you went on and on about how good it was?"

Now I know what you're thinking. And yes, we had actually gone by and visited Ms. Mable after the wake to take her a plate of food.

Wow! Grandmommy had pulled a fast one on me. And there she sat, smiling at me like the cat that swallowed the canary. I discovered later that she was testing me to see if I'd keep my promise or spill the beans. It had been pretty risky of Grandmommy to try that stunt.

I must have passed the test, because I didn't start nursery school until the following year and the whole "pulling a dead girl out of her casket" fiasco was never spoken of again.

FIVE

The Truth May Set
You Free Eventually...
but First it Could Get
You a Spanking!

The Truth May Set You Free Eventually…
but First it Could Get You a Spanking!

Up to that moment, in the bathroom with Mommy staring down at me, her hands placed firmly on her hips, it had never occurred to me to lie. Life had been fine until then. School was fun; I was making friends and even learning a few things. So I couldn't believe I was moments away from being spanked for no good reason.

It had all started when I handed Mommy my report card. I always handed her my report card. I had nothing to hide. I liked school and I was very good at socializing without getting caught by my teacher, Ms. Wells. The entire class liked Ms. Wells because she was a new teacher. "Fresh meat!" In the beginning, Ms. Wells had tried so hard to be nice and fair to us. So we rewarded her by driving her crazy!

It was fun to flash my Little Liverpool smile and squirm my way out of trouble. "Yes Ms. Wells, I promise not to throw any more spitballs in class, ever again."

I think she was beginning to catch on though. Her smile seemed to be turning into some other kind of expression I couldn't quite put my finger on.

So what on earth did this report card say that had my mommy ready to blow a gasket? Beads of sweat were popping up all over my forehead and my heart was galloping like a horse. I bet if you looked real close, you could have seen my heart trying to burst through my chest. Maybe Mommy could see it too! Maybe if she could see that my little heart was about to burst she'd fall to her knees, scoop me into her arms and vow never to strike me again.

I was jerked back to reality when Mommy grabbed my arm, glaring at me. She seemed to be waiting for an answer but what was the question? The last two minutes were a total blur 'cause I was in fantasy land. Whenever I was in trouble or feeling anxious, I'd take myself on a quiet journey to fantasy land.

Mommy probably thought I was stalling. "Did you hear me, young lady? Why did the teacher mark you absent on Thursday, October 14th?"

"I don't know, Mommy. I was in school."

For a moment, Mommy seemed to be thrown off guard by my sincere tone. Her face jumped from one emotion to another. Finally, after a deep sigh she gave me a look of frustration, whipped my report card out from behind her back and held it within inches of my nose. "Your teacher, Ms. Wells, marked you absent on Thursday. Where were you?"

I felt like Bambi must have felt the moment the hunter shot his poor mother. What was Mommy talking about? I always went to school. I never skipped; I was only seven years old. Where was I gonna go? I wasn't one of those "fast" girls that acted as if they could do whatever they wanted. They stuck together anyway and were usually trying to beat me up every chance they got.

I didn't know what to say but looking at my mommy's face I knew I had to say something and all I could think of… was the truth. "Mommy, I was in school. I never miss school. I like school."

"Then why would Ms. Wells mark you absent?"

That was a good question: why would she mark me absent? Maybe she made a mistake? Wait a minute! Maybe this was payback for all those times I had acted up in class while pretending to be so innocent. But grownups didn't do things like that, did they?

Once again, the sound of Mommy's voice brought me back from fantasy land and into the bathroom. The bathroom was Mommy's favorite place to whip me. Maybe that's why my toes seem to curl every time I go to the bathroom now.

"Susan! Did you hear me? Why would she mark you absent if you weren't absent?"

"Mommy, I don't know why. I promise I was there. Maybe she made a mistake."

"Susan, how could this be a mistake? She's never marked you

absent before. She knows who you are. The class is not that big. It's not like she didn't see you."

Those were all great points. I needed somebody like Perry Mason to ask my teacher those very questions. I was sure if Mr. Mason had her on the witness stand she'd break down and admit that indeed, she had made a mistake. "Your honor," Perry would then say, "I request charges be dismissed against Little Liverpool at once!" The judge would strike his gavel and say, "Little Liverpool, charges are dismissed. You are free to go." There would be an outburst of cheering in the courtroom. Mommy would run to throw her arms around me but I'd brush her aside as I'd casually walk from the courtroom, leaving her to cry and beg my forgiveness.

I returned from fantasy land just in time to feel the sting of Mommy's hand across my bottom. "Diane, why do you keep ignoring me?"

When Mommy started using my middle name instead of Susan, things had really gone down the toilet. My trips to fantasy land were about to cost me my life! It was time to do something. "Mommy, I'm telling the truth. I promise! Ms. Wells must have made a mistake. I was in school. I promise!"

Then my mother spoke the words that would change the way I looked at her and all grownups for a long time to come. "Diane, I don't believe you. Ms. Wells didn't make a mistake. She's your teacher. You played hooky from school that day. Now, where did you go and what did you do?"

I stared at my mommy in disbelief. She didn't believe me, her own daughter. She believed a stranger over me. You mean to tell me teachers can't make mistakes? I felt completely deflated, like a pin had been stuck into my chest. Well, what else was there to say? Mommy didn't believe me. She didn't believe me! Tears began dripping down my cheeks and sliding into my mouth. They tasted salty. Then my nose got into the act and down came the snot. I hung my head. Then my knees started shaking, 'cause I knew what was coming.

Mommy grabbed my arm with one hand and started spanking me with the other. I began my dance, jumping and twisting this way and that, to avoid those licks. I noticed the more I jumped the more she missed. But that only made her madder, so she threw me over her knee and went to town on my behind. I had to think of something quick!

"Wait mommy wait!" I yelled. She stopped, her hand poised in midair. Wow, this was good. But what was I going to say now? I took a deep breath and started talking. "Okay, Mommy, I'll tell the truth. I'll tell you what I did on Thursday."

She let me up and I stood there in front of her straightening out my skirt and wiping away the tears and snot from my face. I was trying to buy some time. The truth wasn't working, so whatever I was about to say was gonna have to be good.

"I'm waiting," she said.

"Well you see Mommy, instead of going to school I went to the candy store and then I lost track of time."

"Go on," she said.

Okay, this seemed to be working, but Mommy was no fool. This story needed to get bigger and better in a hurry. "Well, so then, Mommy, I ate some more candy and then I talked to my friends and then the next thing I knew school was over and it was time to go home."

Before I could blink, I was back across her lap being spanked again. Each word was accented by a whack on my behind.

"Do you think I'm stupid or something?"

"Okay, okay, Mommy," I cried. "I'll tell you the truth right now."

Well, I won't bore you with the gory details, but that story took more twists and turns than a roller coaster ride. Mommy grilled me worse than Perry Mason. Even Perry would have wept like a baby by the time my mommy got through with him. Finally, I was done with my story. I stared at Mommy. She stared at me. After what seemed like an eternity, her eyes narrowed into little slits and she said in the most scary tone I'd ever heard, "Don't you ever lie to me or miss school again, do you hear me?"

"Yes, Mommy, I promise."

Her voice had me frozen. What else was I going to say? I was seven years old, she was a grown up and she had won.

Later that evening while lying in bed sucking my thumb, (which always made me feel better and helped me sort things out) I decided, it didn't matter if you lied or told the truth, you just couldn't win. The best thing to do was to try and say whatever these grownups wanted to hear. So I drifted off to sleep, dreaming of the day I'd be grown and nobody could ever tell me what to do again. The next day at school as I walked into class, Ms. Wells said her usual, "Good morning, Susan."

I just looked at her and rolled my eyes. I couldn't believe she had the nerve to be so cheerful and everything after she had nearly destroyed my life. When I didn't respond, she looked puzzled and said, "Susan, are you alright? I said good morning to you."

"Yes, Ms. Wells, I heard you. I'm sorry."

Suddenly, my face felt hot as tears welled up in my eyes. I was thinking about that spanking from the night before.

"Susan, what's wrong? Why are you crying?" She bent down to look at me more closely.

That was it. I couldn't hold myself back any longer and I let her have it. "Ms. Wells, why did you mark me absent from school on my report card? I never miss school, Ms. Wells."

"Oh my, well, let me look in my book. What day was it?" She walked over to her desk, thumbed through the book and said, "Oh no, there must be some mistake. You were here on Thursday. Remember, we had the assembly that afternoon and you were hall monitor."

I knew it! Grownups do make mistakes. Hah! She even admitted it!

"Susan would you like me to call your mother and straighten this out?"

Was she kidding? Of course I would! This woman had no clue. Because of her I had experienced more pain and suffering in one night than I had endured in my entire seven years on earth. But she was a grownup, so instead I said, "Yes, ma'am, thank you, Ms. Wells." Boy, if only I were a grownup!

That evening, Mommy made me my favorite meal, a big, juicy hamburger with homemade French fries and a Coca Cola strawberry ice cream float. This treat was usually reserved for Saturday nights. Ms. Wells must have called and cleared things up.

As I was enjoying my hamburger, Mommy cleared her throat.

"Susan," she said in what sounded like her "I'm sorry" voice, "Ms. Wells called me today and apologized for the mistake she made on your report card."

I stared at the French fry I was twirling between my fingers. I wasn't gonna say anything just yet. I was gonna milk this baby for all it was worth.

"Susan, Mommy is so sorry she didn't believe you. Can you ever forgive me?"

I didn't say a word and I could tell that my silence was making her squirm. Mommy took a deep breath and kept talking.

"Listen, honey, Mommy promises if something like this ever happens again I will always give you the benefit of the doubt until I check it out with your teacher, okay?"

"Okay, Mommy." I made sure I sounded really pitiful. I think she got the point 'cause she smiled and put more French fries on my plate.

After that, something changed between Mommy and me. A line had been drawn in the sand and it was now me on one side and the grownups on the other. I did say, "Okay, Mommy, I forgive you," like I was supposed to, but I didn't see how I was ever gonna get over that spanking or the fact that she hadn't trusted me.

Over the next few months Mommy did everything she could to show me that she trusted me completely and in time all was well between us. That is until that day I signed her name to my report card. But that's another story.

Six

Me, Grandmommy and
My First Fist Fight

Me, Grandmommy and My First Fist Fight

It was the fall of 1957 when I started noticing a lot of things about people. First, I noticed that people weren't really just Black or White. People came in many shades and colors. In my family, Mommy was a rich, chewy caramel color like one of my favorite candies, Mary Jane's. Granddaddy was like the dark brown color of his favorite Alaga syrup. Grandmommy was the shade of rich dark cocoa. I was closer to Mommy's color, and that was fine with me. But I was beginning to notice that for some people being a lighter shade was thought to be better than being darker.

I don't remember when I first noticed that. Maybe it started with television. Everybody on TV was white. I never saw anybody that looked like me except Amos and Andy, and they acted very different than any Negroes I knew. I liked the show but sometimes I felt they acted silly and stupid. Years later, though, I realized they couldn't have been that stupid since they had somehow managed to get themselves a TV show. Mommy didn't like the show but my grandparents loved it. They'd laugh and shake their heads at the jokes and antics of Amos, Andy and Sapphire. I guess, for them, seeing any Negroes on TV was better than no Negroes on TV at all.

I was beginning to hear and notice so many confusing things about what white people and colored people thought about each other. For instance, I often heard that white people thought all Negroes looked alike. They couldn't have been looking very closely because I don't think I ever saw two Negroes that looked exactly alike, ever! But I guess, for most white people, the point was, who wanted to spend their time looking closely at Negroes? It seemed kind of sad to me that white folks didn't want to get to know us because as far as I was concerned there was nothing more fun than being with my crazy family, especially when we were all gathered around the dining room table eating Grandmommy's cooking, laughing and having a good old time.

A good old time was not what I was having when each day I had to leave the coziness of my home and go out into the world of school, teachers, making friends and everything else that was new and strange.

For one thing, I had to deal with remembering how to get to and from school every day without getting lost even though school was only three blocks away. Then there was the scary job of figuring out how to avoid being chased, captured and eaten by one of the many stray dogs that ran around the neighborhood looking for fearful little six-year-olds to terrorize. Mostly, dogs would be minding their own business until they got wind of me running the other way, screaming my head off. No matter how many times Grandmommy told me, "Diane, they only chase you when you run, so stop running and they won't chase you, for heaven's sake," it did no good. I couldn't seem to help myself. The minute I saw a dog I started running and screaming.

As a result, I could out run just about any dog I came across. They'd chase me into one of the many unlocked vestibules I had discovered on my travels to and from school. I was the embarrassment of my family and the talk of my entire neighborhood. People would say, "Why, you haven't lived until you've seen that Little Liverpool run!" "That child is the fastest little streak of chocolate lightning with pig tails you ever did see!" And I'm sure as far as those little dogs were concerned there was no better thrill for them than chasing me around the block.

As if that weren't enough, there were neighborhood kids I had to deal with. One of them lived across the street from me. She and her family were among the handful of whites still living on our block. Grandmommy said they were German.

There was something about the way she said "German" that made me think German people were to be feared and avoided. I was discovering that just like Negroes came in all shades of brown, white people came from all kinds of backgrounds. There were German white people, Italian white people and Polish white people and what they all seemed to have in common was that they did not like Negroes. A lot of this was never talked about out loud. That's the way it was with grown folks, you had to figure out what was behind the words. Grownups always spoke in code, especially when they were trying to hide something. Figuring out what they were talking about was what I lived for!

One day, as I was passing this German girl's house, I looked up and noticed she was watching me from her front porch. As I got closer, she began singing in a low, soft voice, "Nigger, nigger, nigger." I had never heard the word "nigger" before, and since she was smiling as she sang, I thought it was some goofy German song. So I smiled and waved, which was my way of saying thank you for the song. This caused her to burst into laughter as she ran into the house calling out to her mother. I could hear her say, "Mama, Mama—," The rest of what she said must have been in German but I did hear that word "nigger" again. So I just assumed she was thrilled to have found someone that seemed to enjoy her little German song as much as she did.

Since home was only three blocks from school, home was where I had my lunch. Having lunch with Grandmommy was one of my favorite things in the whole wide world. I'd eat and hum while she watched her soap operas. So I decided to tell Grandmommy about my run-in with the German girl.

I should have known better. Grandmommy was a "take no prisoners" kind of woman. She was clearly ahead of her time. Grandmommy would say she didn't know why she wasn't dead 'cause all her life she had never been afraid to let anybody, colored or white, have a piece of her mind. I guess that's why God decided the best way to keep Grandmommy alive was to steer her away from as many white folks as possible.

"Grandmommy—"

"Yes, baby."

"What's a 'nigger'?"

"Who called you a 'nigger'?" she yelled.

My heart skipped a beat as I watched Grandmommy gear up for a "conniption fit" (that was the word we used back then to describe someone who was about to go off the deep end). What did I do? How did she know somebody had called me a 'nigger'? And why all of a sudden was she getting so upset over this word? This must be a very bad word. Now I was really scared. I felt I was on trial just like on the Perry Mason show when the person on the witness stand was ready to crack and spill their guts in the final climatic scene.

"Who called you a 'nigger'?" she demanded again. "Come on now, tell Grandmommy, who it was?"

I swallowed the lump stuck in my throat and noticed my mouth was as dry as sandpaper. I could hear my voice crack as I began to speak. "Well, Grandmommy, you see that German girl across the street was singing to me as I walked past her house."

"Go on. What was she singing?"

I watched my grandmommy's face as I carefully thought about what I would say next. Grandmommy already seemed to know where this story was going. She looked as if she were moments away from exploding. Her eyes had narrowed and she was working her mouth and jaw like she did when she was about to unleash her fury.

"Well, Grandmommy, I thought she was singing a German song. I thought 'nigger' was a German word."

"So she called you a 'nigger'?" Grandmommy screamed.

Uh oh, here we go. At that moment, Grandmommy looked as if she was about to have a heart attack. I could imagine smoke coming out the top of her head. She jumped up from the table, something I had never seen her do before. Most of the time, it took her a full minute to stand up. Each move she made was usually accompanied by a moan, a groan or a "Lord, have mercy." But not today!

She headed for the living room, grabbing her cane on the way. She used it to open the shade as she peered out the window in the direction of the German girl's house. Thank goodness, she didn't see the girl. Knowing Grandmommy, she would have leaned out of the window, waving her cane, yelling, cursing and threatening to kill the girl. How embarrassing that would have been! Grandmommy was "fit to be tied" (another one of her favorite expressions). I had never seen her act like this before.

By now I was crying, trembling and ready to pee on myself. Something bad was going to happen to that girl for calling me that word and it was all my fault! Why hadn't I kept my mouth shut? I knew how crazy Grandmommy could be.

Hearing my sobs got Grandmommy's attention and finally she began to calm down. "Come here, Diane," she said, as we settled onto the sofa. I snuggled up close to her and nuzzled my head against her soft, warm bosom and continued crying. It was a relief to cry. Maybe my being upset would take Grandmommy's mind away from going across the street to beat the little German girl.

55

I quieted myself and began sucking my thumb, something I did whenever I felt upset or confused. Grandmommy gently pulled my thumb out of my mouth and began wiping away my tears with the handkerchief she always kept in her housecoat pocket. She caressed my face in her large, soft hands and drew me close until our noses were almost touching.

"Listen child," she said, in a soft voice. "The word 'nigger' is a word white folks use to try and break your spirit. Baby, that girl was mockin' you."

Mockin' me? Wow, was I a sucker! I guess it was pretty funny to see me smile and wave back at her like that.

"Now, Diane, I know your mommy don't approve of you gettin' into fights and all, but sometimes you just can't let people get away with things like this. The next time she calls you that word you better beat the slop out of her, you hear me? You ball up your little fist and you let her have it!" She balled up her own fist and punched at the air like a boxer to show me what she meant.

I don't think Grandmommy was ever gonna be a member of

the nonviolence movement. That was where she and my mommy parted company. Grandmommy believed a little "rough justice" was just what the doctor ordered. But in my heart I wanted to be nonviolent just like Mommy, but Mommy didn't go to school with me every day. She wasn't there to protect me and I didn't have any brothers or sisters that could help me out. I was on my own.

So I said, "Yes, Grandmommy," as I knew I was supposed to. But I didn't want to get into a fight with that German girl or anybody else for that matter. I was too afraid I'd be the one to get beat up. Why couldn't Grandmommy go beat up the girl herself since that word upset her so much? I knew better than to ask that question though.

I had been given my marching orders. It was time to strike a blow for freedom, the "race" and myself. But all I wanted to do was to watch Captain Kangaroo and forget about this whole mess. Was I going to have to beat up everybody that called me a 'nigger'? It seemed to be a popular word among white folks from what Grandmommy was telling me. If that was the case, I was gonna be one very busy fist-fightin' Little Liverpool.

Every day after that I prayed I wouldn't run into that German girl or any other white person, for that matter. White people were now the enemy, to be avoided at all costs.

About a week later, I was walking home from school when I heard that familiar voice behind me singing, "Nigger, nigger, nigger!"

My heart jumped into my throat then dropped to my stomach. I tried to pretend I didn't see her but that made her even more determined. The faster I walked the faster she walked. The more I tried to ignore her, the louder she sang. Where was Grandmommy when I needed her? My palms began to sweat. I was breathing so fast and hard I thought I was going to pass out. The time had come to take a stand, but I was so afraid. What if she turned out to be stronger than I was and ended up beating the crap out of me? I saw Grandmommy's disappointed face flash before my eyes. If I didn't take on this girl I'd never hear the end of it. I'd rather take my chances with this German girl than face the wrath of my grandmommy!

With my fist balled up and ready to go, I steadied my nerves, took a deep breath, closed my eyes and spun around with all my might. Much to my surprise, both my fists collided right into her chest and stomach. I opened my eyes, amazed to see that because she had been following me so closely, my sudden move had caught her by surprise, nearly causing her to fall over backward.

I looked down in wonder at my fists as if I were seeing them for the very first time. I opened my mouth to try and speak but nothing came out. She was busy holding her stomach, moaning and groaning in what seemed to be great pain. Her eyes were wild with fear as she stared at me in disbelief.

I could feel my knees knocking together as I continued to clench my fists and brace myself for round two. I was certain she was going to come charging back at me with everything she had. Instead, she slowly backed away, never taking her eyes off me. She spun around and ran for home. She was crying, screaming and muttering something in what was probably German. Wow! She was as afraid of me as I was of her. Imagine that! I guess under the skin we were not so different after all.

I looked up in the sky to see if God had been watching me. I didn't see him anywhere. Grandmommy said God saw and heard everything I did, especially when I was away from her watchful eye. So I closed my eyes, folded my hands in prayer and promised God I would never fight again. As it turns out, that was a very short-lived promise. I'm sure God was somewhere shaking his head in disappointment. But God was up there and Grandmommy was down here and down here was where I had to live!

Seven

The Ludens Wild Cherry Cough Drop Incident

The Ludens Wild Cherry Cough Drop Incident

Anyone who's ever eaten a Ludens Wild Cherry cough drop understands why I couldn't help myself. First of all, there's just something about that luscious red color and that sweet cherry flavor as it curls around your tongue and glides down your throat like syrup. You can't eat just one. If a person was only meant to eat one wild cherry cough drop they would have wrapped and sold each one separately. But they didn't. They sold them in that black and white box with those two "Abe Lincoln" look-alikes facing each other, so proper and dignified-looking.

We kids knew the game though. We weren't stupid. Those cough drops had nothing to do with having a cough. Ludens Wild Cherry cough drops were candy, pure and simple. You didn't eat them because you have a cough, although that would have been a great excuse. You ate them because they tasted good.

So the events of that Saturday afternoon could not have been a surprise to anyone. There I was with my beloved granddaddy, working as his assistant at his newsstand concession at the elevated train station on 63rd and University Avenue. I always perched on Granddaddy's stool so I could see everything and have quick and easy access to all the candy and gum. Watching the people rush through on their way to the trains was my second favorite thing to do. Number one, of course, was eating as much as I could without throwing up.

Every time I "worked" with Granddaddy it was like Christmas. How he made any money was a mystery to me. On the days I was there I'm sure I ate my weight in candy and soda pop.

My granddaddy was a quiet, gentle man who never seemed to be in a hurry no matter what was happening. As if on cue, a crowd of people would rush to his newsstand just as the train was pulling up to the station. Granddaddy worked alone and could only wait on one person at a time. I was just learning how to count so I was of no help. People would take advantage of this by waiting for the train to pull up then grabbing what they wanted without paying and jumping on the train just before the doors closed.

His regular customers always paid. If the line was long, they'd take what they wanted and leave their money. Granddaddy didn't seem to mind. As a matter of fact, he didn't seem to mind about much of anything. Granddaddy was like a turtle. He walked slow, talked slow, ate slow and dressed slow. Grandmommy would often joke that Granddaddy took longer to get dressed than any woman. Every Saturday morning Granddaddy and I would leave for the newsstand, hand in hand, and every Saturday morning Mommy and Grandmommy would say as we headed out the door, "Granddaddy, don't let Diane eat everything in sight!" But Granddaddy was no match for the cunning ways of Little Liverpool. It'd be time to close up the newsstand and I'd say in my sweetest, most syrupy voice, "Granddaddy, can I have just one more…..?" You fill in the blank. It didn't matter what it was 'cause I had probably eaten five of them already. So he'd give in and I'd stuff one more thing down my throat. The "one more thing" I wanted before we left for home was, you guessed it, Ludens Wild Cherry cough drops.

By the time we got home I had eaten the entire box. Yummy! I had to eat the whole box on the way because I had nowhere to hide them and if Mommy had seen them she'd have taken them away from me and fussed at Granddaddy. So you see, I had to protect Granddaddy by eating the whole box.

Since Mommy and I lived downstairs and my grandparents lived upstairs, spending the night with Granddaddy and Grandmommy on the weekends was almost like going on vacation. It was Saturday so as usual, I prepared to spend the night with them. I loved my grandparents. They let me do pretty much whatever I wanted.

Like drinking coffee for example. It was a secret late-night ritual. If Mommy had known I was drinking coffee (and she probably did), she might have stopped letting me spend the night with them. Granddaddy would let me sit on his lap and drink out of his cup. Wow! Coffee was so good and I felt so grown up sipping and talking, even though I always had the feeling they weren't really listening to me.

Coffee without cream and sugar tasted like medicine to me. Grandmommy drank her coffee "straight." She loved to say, "Diane, you and Granddaddy aren't real coffee drinkers like me;

you all just like a little coffee in your cream and sugar." That was okay with us. Nobody was gonna argue that Grandmommy couldn't "hold" her coffee.

Well, it was time for bed. Grandmommy helped me bathe, then showered me with talcum powder until I looked like a ghost. She knelt with me as I said my prayers and helped me climb into bed. And I do mean climb. The bed I slept in when I spent the night

was not only big; it seemed to be five feet off the floor.

Sometimes I'd ask Grandmommy to lie next to me until I fell asleep and she would. I'd curl up close to her soft warm body and drift off to sleep. Later that night I woke with a funny feeling in my stomach. Suddenly, before I knew what was happening, I threw up all over myself and Grandmommy who had been snoring peacefully beside me. That horrible sound you make when you throw up startled her to life as she fumbled to turn on the lamp.

"Wha…what's going on Diane? Oh, my goodness, what on earth?"

It took a second or two for Grandmommy to focus but the smell left no doubt what had happened. "Diane, are you all right?" I have never understood why the first thing people ask after something bad happens to you is "Are you all right?" It seemed pretty obvious to me that I wasn't all right.

At first Grandmommy thought I had thrown up blood, but she quickly realized what it really was. "Diane, did you eat cough drops today?"

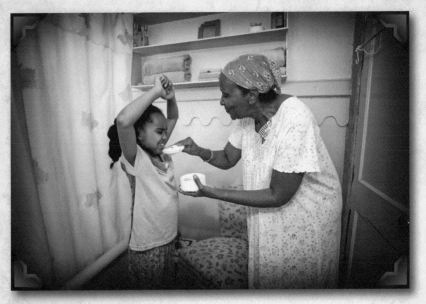

"Yes, ma'am."

"How many times have we told you eatin' all that junk is gonna make you sick?"

"Yes, ma'am."

There was nothing to say. She was right. But why did grownups think that because they had warned you not to do something you were actually going to stop doing it? Especially if it was fun?

The thing I will always remember about that night though is how gently, lovingly and patiently Grandmommy cleaned up all the mess. Then re-bathed me, re-applied talcum powder all over me and climbed back into bed with me. As she turned out the light, we both let out a deep sigh as we drifted off to sleep—again.

Next thing I knew, I was waking up with that same funny feeling. Then there it came again like a rushing river pouring over me and Grandmommy. I could hear Grandmommy in the darkness let out a deep sigh followed by a weary "Lord, have mercy," as she reached for the light.

That was the last Saturday I ever went to work with Granddaddy. I had been fired!

EIGHT

Me, Grandmommy and
the Pickens Floral Club

Me, Grandmommy and the Pickens Floral Club

Another of my favorite things to do on a Saturday was to tag along with Grandmommy to her monthly meetings of the Pickens Floral Club of Chicago, Illinois. The club got its name from the fact that most of the members were born in Pickens County, Mississippi.

They were a wonderful, lively and sometimes rowdy bunch of folks. The Club did a lot of great things for the community such as raising money for charities and visiting the sick. But I think their main reason for being a club was so they could enjoy each others' company, eat, fuss and gossip.

Every year they held a Mothers' Day Tea which was always a lot of fun. I never understood why they called it a Tea. I never saw any tea; hot, cold or otherwise. Just like I never knew where the Floral in Pickens Floral Club came from. I think they just liked the way it sounded. Whenever I asked about these things, my questions went unanswered. Grown folks felt that little people like me shouldn't ask so many questions.

The Club had a president, a treasurer and a secretary. They even had a sergeant-at-arms, a very old man named Mr. McAfee. He must have been at least 60. He had been sergeant-at-arms since the club was born nearly 30 years before. I used to wonder what he would have done if those old ladies had gotten into a real fight 'cause it took him ten minutes just to stand up. Every meeting he'd sit in his favorite chair and nod off until it was time to eat.

I loved going to those club meetings for two reasons. First of all, I was Mattie Lou's granddaughter, so that made me kind of the club mascot. All the members fussed over me because I was the only little person that tagged along with their grandmothers to those meetings. Second, the home-cooked food was probably the best in Chicago.

When Grandmommy and I would arrive at the home of a club

member, the first thing I'd do is run into the dining room to look at all the many dishes everyone had brought. Even though I was barely tall enough to see over the edge of the table, I'd get as close I could then inhale all the wonderful aromas and fantasize about which foods I would eat. I couldn't wait! Then Grandmommy would come and snatch me away from the table.

The club meeting always started with a song, usually "What a Friend We Have in Jesus." Most of the ladies couldn't sing a lick. In fact, it seemed as though the worse they sounded the louder they sang. Sometimes I'd sing along too and if I didn't know the words, I'd just hum.

Then there was the boring part of the meeting; old business, new business... All I could think of at that point was, when would this be over so I could eat?

Sometimes there'd be fights (or discussions as Grandmommy would call them). Those were always fun to watch. I'd cross my legs Indian style and get myself a ringside seat. The discussion would begin calmly with everyone being nice and polite, following the rules of order. Then things would get heated and all the ladies would whip out their church fans. You could have probably stirred up a tornado with all the air blowin' around in that room. From there it was downhill all the way. Everybody started shouting, mainly because they couldn't hear that well. Somebody would accuse somebody else of being forgetful, which to an old person was the worst thing you could say.

Then it was a free for all! The "rules of order" went right out the window. Hats started comin' off, wigs turned every which-a-way then finally somebody would wake up Mr. Sergeant-at-arms. It would take him a couple of minutes to figure out what was going on. He'd start coughing, hoping to get everyone's attention. If that didn't work, he'd cough a little louder.

It was usually my grandmommy that could get everyone to calm down. She'd start by humming a tune and soon everyone would join in. Then they'd all agree to table the "discussion" for later and bring it up as old business at the next meeting. Of course, there was the latest gossip to be discussed and who had the scoop on whom.

Finally, the closing song, followed by the benediction and then off to the dining room. I never had to wait in line to get my food. Grandmommy would fix my plate. "Diane, what do you want?" she'd say. "Everything, Grandmommy!"

"Alright, and you better eat every bit of it."

We both knew that would not be a problem. By the time we left those meetings I usually felt as if I had swallowed a basketball. It was at one of these club meetings that I learned an important lesson: saying what you think is not always the best way to go. After everyone had finished eating, one of the ladies started passing around a picture of her newest grandson. I wanted to see the picture too but I couldn't get close enough. Every time it came my way I'd lean in hoping for a good look. I even tried to be polite and said,

"May I see, please?" just like Grandmommy and Mommy had taught me. But for some reason they kept passing that picture over my head, keeping it just out of my reach.

I was getting more and more frustrated by the minute, jumping and scrambling around trying to see. I didn't usually have such a problem. What was going on? Finally, I resorted to the only thing I knew that always worked. I started crying. I had crying down to an art. Still no reaction. This was very unusual. It was time to pull out all the stops. I stomped my foot and began yelling, "Why can't I see that picture?"

The ladies continued to ignore me as they passed around the picture, laughing and cooing over that darn baby. I squeezed myself into Grandmommy's chair and pretended to go to sleep, all the while watching the action out of the corner of my eye. I could see the picture making its way toward Grandmommy, so just before she got it, I reached out and grabbed it. A hush settled over the room. Grandmommy snatched the picture away from me but I had seen enough to know why they had so careful avoided letting me look at it.

There was something wrong with the baby's face. They had kept the picture away from me because they knew I would look at that baby's picture and say exactly what I was thinking.

What happened next could have scarred me for life. I was about to say, "Grandmommy, what's wrong with that baby's face?" Grandmommy clamped one hand over my mouth and began laughing hysterically as she passed the picture to the next person. Everyone took their cue from this and began laughing loudly as well. The lady whose grandson's picture they were passing around looked puzzled but joined in too, maybe thinking she'd missed something. Grandmommy had very large hands and I'm sure she just meant to cover my mouth, but in her haste to shut me up, she covered both my nose and mouth.

I couldn't believe my very own grandmommy was trying to smother me to death! I began kicking, wiggling and jerking around in her lap. But it was no use. Finally, in desperation, I bit her hand as hard as I could. She yelled and took her hand away.

Again, a hush fell over the room as everyone braced themselves, waiting to hear what I was going to say next. I was busy gasping for air as I turned to face Grandmommy.

When she looked down at my face she must have realized what she had done. She quickly pressed me to her bosom and said, "Oh, baby, Grandmommy is so sorry. I didn't mean to hurt you. I squeezed you too tight, didn't I? Come on; let me take you to the bathroom." Now I was really confused. Did I need to go to the bathroom? I didn't feel like I had to go. I completely forgot about the baby picture as she carried me off to the bathroom. What in the world had just happened in there? By the time we got into the bath room I had calmed down. I placed my hands on my hips and did my best to look hurt and angry.

"Grandmommy, why'd you—"

"Diane, hold on a minute." She sat me down on a small stool.

"Listen, child, I'm sorry I held my hand over your mouth so tight you couldn't breathe but I was tryin' to stop you from saying how ugly that baby was."

"Wow, Grandmommy! How did you know that's what I was thinking?"

"I know you baby. Listen, if you had said, 'This baby's ugly,' how do you think that would have made the baby's grandmother feel?"

I had to admit, I'd never thought about that.

"Diane, it's time for you to start learnin' how to think about other people's feelings before you open your mouth. Now, just so you know, there's something wrong with that baby's mouth. It's called 'cleft palate.' Now, I don't expect you to understand what that is but I do expect you to keep your mouth shut about it when we go back into that room, you hear me?"

"Yes, ma'am."

"Diane, don't you dare embarrass me in front of my friends or I'm gonna whip you, do you understand me?"

"Yes, ma'am."

Whip me? Grandmommy had never whipped me before. She had never even threatened to do such a thing. Something about the look in her eyes though, told me this was no joke.

"Now, straighten out your face and let's go."

We walked out of the bathroom hand in hand as if nothing had happened. Everyone could tell by the look on Grandmommy's face that she had straightened me out and there was nothing to worry about.

As they were leaving, each club member kissed me on the cheek and gave me a wink. It was as if they were saying, "Don't worry baby, it's gonna be alright."

Boy oh boy, was I really gonna have to start thinking before I spoke? Where was the fun in that? Oh well! I guess learning to think before I spoke was gonna be like when I had to swallow castor oil every winter. It was awful going down but in the long run, it was supposed to be good for me.

Family Photo Album

Grandmommy
&
Granddaddy

Mommy

"Little Liverpool"

Me

What are your "Diary Stories?"

Have fun!

The_____Diaries

_____
_____
_____
_____
_____
_____
_____
_____
_____
_____
_____
_____
_____
_____
_____
_____
_____
_____
_____

Special Mention

to

Mr. Willie Watkins
owner of
Willie Watkins Funeral Home

Atlanta, Georgia
and
Symenthia Dearing

for the generous use of their beautiful facilities,

Kathryn Copper
for the gracious use of her beautiful home,

Landmark Education
Thank you for the education, training and development that
empowered me to fulfill my dreams.

ABOUT THE AUTHOR

Susan Diane Liverpool was born and raised on the Southside of Chicago. She is the only child of Dorothy Thomas and Norman John Liverpool. Susan grew up with her grandparents and mother. She attended Hirsch High School and when it became clear that pursuing a dance career was not to be, she decided to become a Registered Nurse. Susan graduated from the University of Illinois with a BSN in Nursing. After graduating, she moved to Atlanta, Georgia, and married. That union produced her only son, Jason Alexander Hill.

Susan loves the Arts. Her vision for the world is that everyone is clear that **"The Arts are a ministry to the Soul."** "My purpose in life is to leave a legacy of art, inspiration and laughter, people coming alive inside the magic of The Arts!"

Susan has published three limited-edition books of poetry. The latest is a collection called Reflections on Life scheduled to be re-released in 2011. She has also written two children's books, The Lion and the Porcupine and The Story of Nappy Hair. Look for these books in 2011 as well.

Susan continues to live in Atlanta, Georgia.

Please visit Susan on her website at: www.thelittleliverpooldiaries.com

10% of the royalties from sales of this book through
December 2011 will go to:

The New Sullivan Fine and Performing Arts Magnet Cluster School
8331 South MacKinaw
Chicago, Illinois 60617

**Look for 'The Little Liverpool Diaries' audio book coming
soon, including original songs written by the author.**

Excerpt from "The Lion and the Porcupine"

By
Susan Liverpool

Coming in 2011

Being King of the Jungle can sometimes be a lonely life. Where do you turn for stimulating conversation? The Pride is always away hunting for food. The other animals are beneath you. You can't be seen talking to a chimpanzee or a crocodile for goodness sake! What would the other animals think?

That's why (just between you and me) I allowed that strange little porcupine with her prickly quills and musty smell to get near me in the first place. I was feeling very vulnerable that afternoon and instead of swatting her with my mighty paw, as I should have, I watched in awe as she slowly and courageously inched her way toward me. How dare she approach the King of the Jungle, sniffing and muttering to herself. Was she insane? Had she not been taught how to behave in the presence of royalty?

If I were seen giving the time of day to this little creature, my reputation would be ruined. Lions from all over the jungle would challenge my authority and try to steal my Pride right from under me. So I growled at her with all the fierceness one would expect from a King of my stature. This seemed to startle the little porcupine, but not enough to make her run and hide. Instead, she just sat trembling, staring up at me with those pitiful, watery eyes.

I remained calm. Then in my most majestic and menacing voice I roared, "Why are you here? Don't you know who I am?" The little porcupine jumped and fell back on her bottom. "Dear King, I mean no harm. Please, don't eat me. I have lost my way."

"You have also lost your mind! I could end your life with one swipe of my mighty paw. Don't you know that?"

"I suppose I should but I was separated from my family when I was born and have been on my own for a very long time. I am still learning the ways of the jungle. When I saw you I thought to myself, 'Here is a mighty and majestic King. He will help me find my family and I'll never be lonely again!'

Can you believe this nutty Porcupine? the King thought. What annoying little creatures. You couldn't get to their succulent meat without getting all those quills stuck in your face and mouth, so it was useless to try to eat them.

"I am King of the jungle, you little idiot! Do you suppose I have time to bother with your petty problems?"

The King thought he should probably just majestically walk away, swatting the pathetic porcupine with his tail, yet her innocent pleas were beginning to tug at his heart. Here they were, two lonely creatures; different and yet the same. But he was King and he definitely could not be sympathetic to a porcupine. So to keep up appearances, he turned his head and yawned to give the impression of being bored with the little rodent.

The King's rude behavior did not deter the porcupine. "Your Majesty, my name is Penelope and if you befriend me I can do you a great service."

"What in heaven's name do you suppose you can do for me? If it weren't for those prickly little quills you carry around on your back I'd have eaten you by now."

"Tee hee hee!" Penelope covered her mouth with her paws as she giggled nervously. "Oh, my King, you are hilarious! You wouldn't really eat me, would you? I've heard that Lions of your caliber don't bother to eat creatures like myself."

Completely exasperated, the King had run out of patience with this pest. The Pride would be returning soon with the day's kill. If they saw him cavorting with a porcupine they'd snatch up their prize and join another Pride. There was nothing more humiliating and shameful than a Lion who couldn't hold onto his "Pride," so to speak.

The king carefully slipped his paw under the porcupine and skillfully flipped her over, exposing her soft pink underbelly. He watched the thing desperately wiggle and squirm, trying to right herself. The king drew close so little Penelope could see his blazing eyes and smell the heat of his breath bearing down on her. His mouth was big enough to swallow her whole.

The King brought forth a vicious growl from the back of his throat. "I'll give you two seconds to tell me why I shouldn't bite into your soft little belly and have you for an appetizer!"

LaVergne, TN USA
30 October 2010
202718LV00001B